The Beatitudes

Coloring and Activity Book

Written by D. Thomas Halpin, FSP

Illustrated by Virginia Helen Richards, FSP

"It's all in the attitude!"

Pauline
BOOKS & MEDIA
Boston

Here's the blueprint for being my friend and finding joy and love in life!

Living my **8 BEATITUDES** will help you to be brave and strong so you'll stay close to me and bring my light to everyone you meet. It's all in the attitude!

The 8 Beatitudes

1. BLESSED are the poor in spirit, for theirs is the kingdom of heaven.

2. BLESSED are those who mourn, for they will be comforted.

3. BLESSED are the meek, for they will inherit the earth.

4. BLESSED are those who hunger and thirst for righteousness, for they will be filled.

5. BLESSED are the merciful, for they will receive mercy.

6. BLESSED are the pure in heart, for they will see God.

7. BLESSED are the peacemakers, for they will be called children of God.

8. BLESSED are those who are persecuted for righteousness' sake, for theirs is the kingdom of heaven.

Matthew 5:3-10

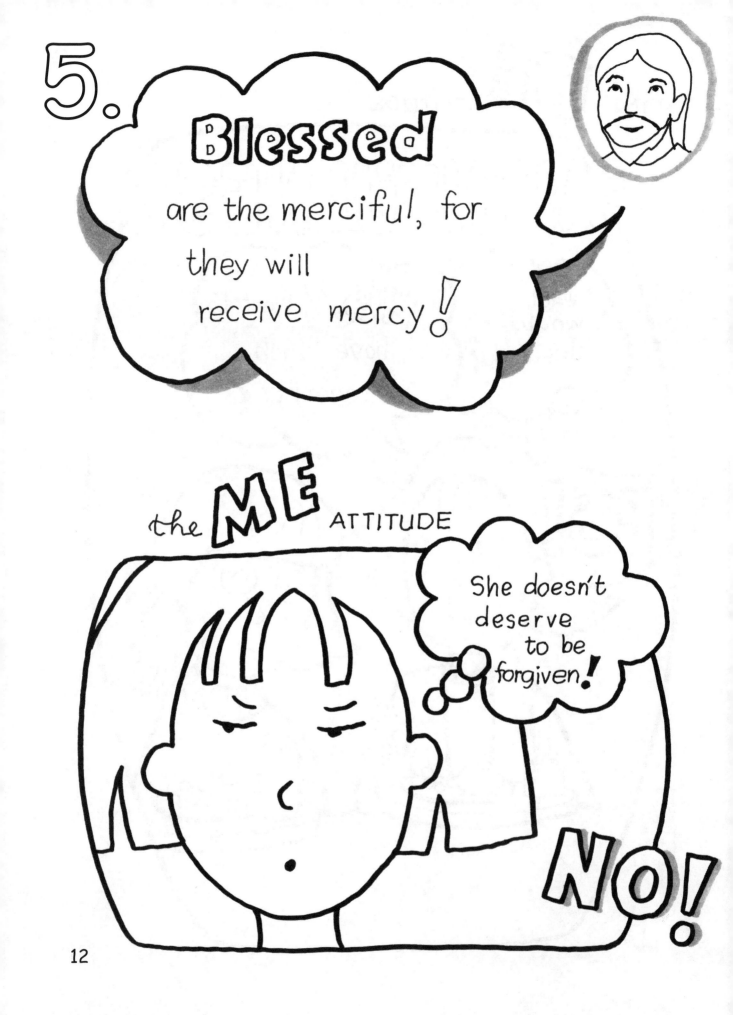

a·MAZE·ing ATTIDUDES!

Help Angel and Maurice find their way through this challenging maze.

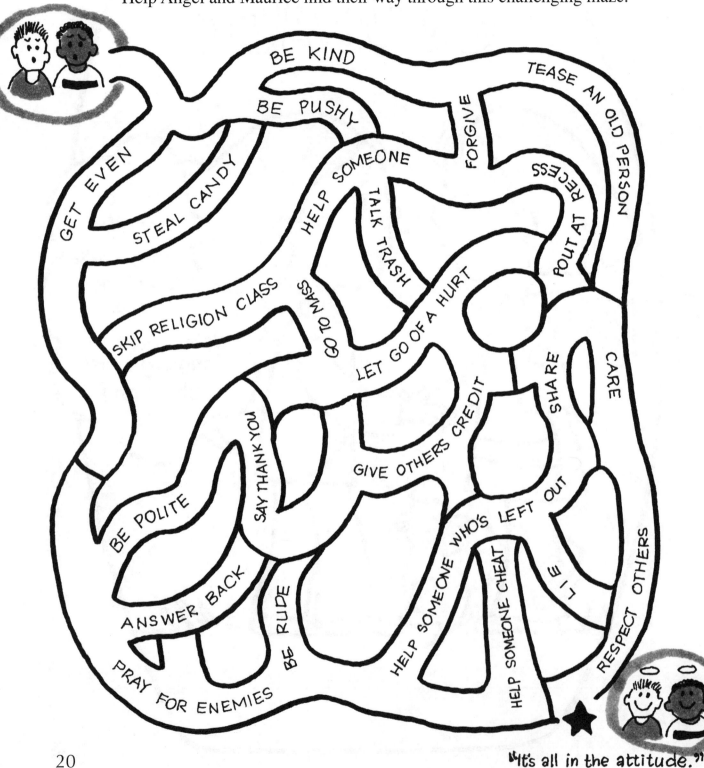

"It's all in the attitude."

dot-to-dot

What is the most important word in the Beatitudes?

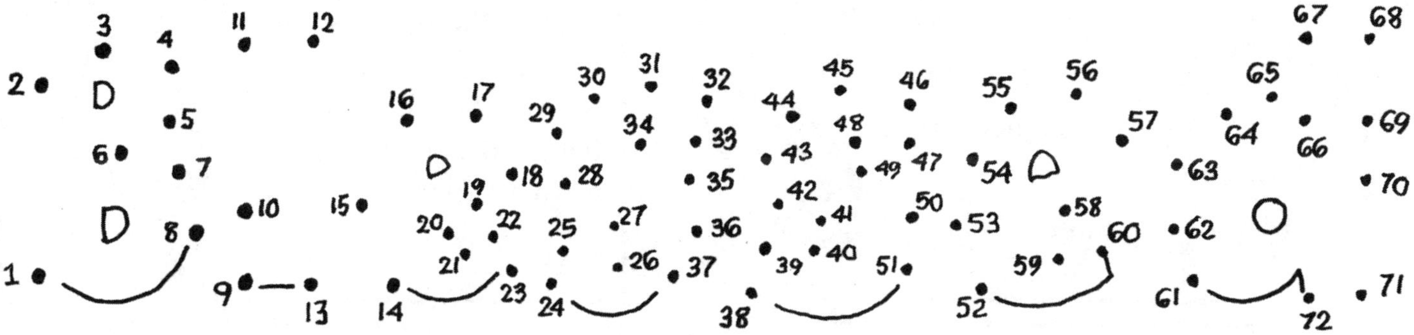

Knock Knock...

Make a Beatitude doorknob hanger for your bedroom!

Pick your favorite Beatitude (check through this book) and letter it on your doorknob hanger.

Cut out

Make your hanger out of: foam, cardboard, poster paper, or felt.

Decorate your hanger with: paints, markers, tassels, glitter, fringe, beads, or jewels.

P.S. Be sure to make the doorknob hole bigger than your doorknob!

The answers to the puzzles on pages 21–24 are on the inside of the back cover.

Blessed are the poor in spirit, for theirs is the kingdom of heaven!
BLESSED are the MEEK for they will inherit the earth!

The BIG 8

Find the right Beatitude for each true-life scene! Write in the page number you found it on!

Marcia needed help to clean her room, so she asked her brother...

Page ___5___

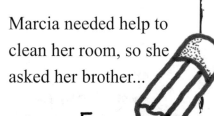

Agnes' friends want her to tease Jimmy, who is in special ed. classes. She wants to be accepted, but she decides to say no to her friends...

Page _____

Dyrell was furious with his Dad for forgetting the game. He asked Dad if they could talk about his feelings...

Page _____

Ron was the most awarded swimmer at the pool. He used his gifts to help other kids out...

Page _____

At the bus stop, Veronica invited Alex to her party, because Alex was afraid to make friends...

Page _____

Marc's brother and sister were arguing over the remote. He decided to referee them and help them compromise...

Page _____

Troy's friends ignored him at lunch because he wouldn't help them cheat. Troy knew it was wrong...

Page _____

At summer camp, no one else seemed to say prayers. Connie made time to pray in bed after lights-out...

Page _____

Hidden Eights!

Jesus gave us the Beatitudes during the Sermon on the Mount. Find how many **8**'s are hidden in this picture.

23

crazy 8's

There's an 8-letter holy word hidden on each octagon. Find the first letter of each word and you'll discover the rest of the word!

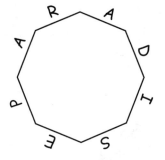

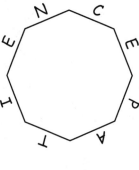

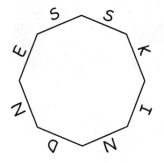

_____   _____   _____

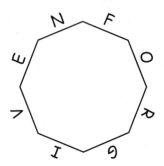

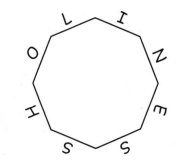

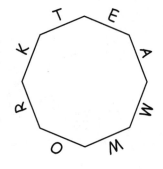

_____   _____   _____

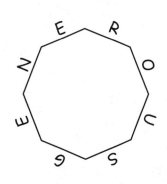

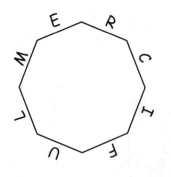

_____   _____